The Anxiety Happens

GUIDED JOURNAL

Write Your Way *to*
Peace *of* Mind

JOHN P. FORSYTH, PhD | GEORG H. EIFERT, PhD

New Harbinger Publications, Inc.

Publisher's Note

NEW HARBINGER PUBLICATIONS is a registered trademark of New Harbinger Publications, Inc.

New Harbinger Publications is an employee-owned company.

Copyright © 2023 by John P. Forsyth and Georg Eifert
New Harbinger Publications, Inc.
5674 Shattuck Avenue
Oakland, CA 94609
www.newharbinger.com

Cover and interior design by Amy Shoup

Acquired by Ryan Buresh

Edited by Marisa Solis

Library of Congress Cataloging-in-Publication Data on file

Printed in the United States of America

25		24		23							
10	9	8	7	6	5	4	3	2	1	First Printing

"The Anxiety Happens Guided Journal is an engaging, intriguing, and spot-on guide to the peace of mind you seek. The book presents powerful skills to help you notice and then allow—rather than avoid—your anxiety, followed by skills to help you do what is important and life-affirming in those anxious moments that hold you back. I recommend this book for anyone who struggles with anxiety."

—Michael A. Tompkins, PhD, ABPP, codirector of the San Francisco Bay Area Center for Cognitive Therapy, and author of *The Anxiety and Depression Workbook*

"If you are someone who loves to journey inward and explore new ways to understand your anxiety and promote recovery, you must read and follow this book. *The Anxiety Happens Guided Journal* is a thoughtful, compassionate way to explore ways to overcome anxiety while living your values and building inner resilience."

—Karen Cassiday, PhD, owner of The Anxiety Treatment Center of Greater Chicago, and author of *Freedom from Health Anxiety* and *The No Worries Guide to Raising Your Anxious Child*

"Simple, practical, powerful! This life-changing book offers a deeply compassionate guide to fundamentally transforming your relationship with anxiety. As you work, step by step, through the beautifully written exercises within these pages, you'll learn how to take the power out of anxiety, and go on to build a rich and fulfilling life, while cultivating genuine peace of mind. Highly recommended!"

—Russ Harris, author of *The Happiness Trap* and *ACT Made Simple*

"If you have tried 'everything' to get rid of anxiety and it still won't go away, *The Anxiety Happens Guided Journal* is for you. Let this interactive journal be your personalized space where you can practice stepping out of the anxiety roundabout and into the life you want."

—**Diana Hill**, author of *The ACT Daily Journal*

"Lots of self-help books can be read, or unread, and left on a shelf. *The Anxiety Happens Guided Journal* is a book for you to use, and to take with you on your life's journey. Living with anxiety is tough, and this beautiful, warm, and straightforward journal can help lighten your load and light the way!"

—**Dennis Tirch, PhD**, author of *The Compassionate-Mind Guide to Overcoming Anxiety*

"If you're tired of constantly fighting anxiety, *The Anxiety Happens Guided Journal* offers you a new way out: stop the battle! Instead, notice your anxiety, allow it, and move on! In this thorough and comprehensive workbook, John Forsyth and Georg Eifert offer exercises to help you to stop seeing anxiety as the enemy and start creating a valued life for yourself. Empowering and compassionate!"

—**Lisa M. Schab, LCSW**, psychotherapist; and author of nineteen self-help books, including *Put Your Anxiety Here* and *The Anxiety Workbook for Teens*

New Harbinger Journals for Change

Research shows that journaling has a universally positive effect on mental health. But in the midst of life's difficulties—such as stress, anxiety, depression, relationship problems, parenting challenges, or even obsessive or negative thoughts—where do you begin? New Harbinger *Journals for Change* combine evidence-based psychology with proven-effective guided journaling techniques to help you make lasting personal change—one page at a time. Written by renowned mental health and wellness experts, *Journals for Change* provide a creative and safe space to process difficult emotions, work through challenges, reflect on what matters, and set intentions for the future.

Since 1973, New Harbinger has published practical, user-friendly self-help books and workbooks to help readers make positive change. Our *Journals for Change* offer the same powerfully effective tools—without ever *feeling* like therapy. If you're committed to improving your mental health, these easy-to-use guided journals can help you take small, actionable steps toward lasting well-being.

For a complete list of journals in our *Journals for Change* series, visit newharbinger.com.

Table of Contents

Part 3: Doing . . .121

Introduction:
You're Not Alone

Many people suffering with anxiety feel utterly alone. You may feel that way too. You may think that your anxiety is so intense that nobody could possibly understand what it's like to feel the way you feel. In a sense, you're right; nobody knows your experience better than you. But that doesn't mean that you're alone in this.

People with anxiety disorders are everywhere. They live in every town, state, and country. Anxiety disorders affect the rich and the poor alike. In fact, anxiety disorders are among the most common of all psychological disorders, affecting up to one-third of the population at some point in their lifetimes.[1] That's about 100 million people in the United States alone. To bring the numbers home, imagine that one day everyone with an anxiety disorder decided to wear a red hat. If that were so, then you'd be hard pressed to go about your day without seeing someone wearing one.

There's no way to escape the simple fact that anxiety is a part of life. The emphasis here is on the word "part"; anxiety is just one piece of the life puzzle. Many people do live well, even with significant anxiety. And they do so often with the same anxieties and fears you may be experiencing. You might be wondering, "How they do that? What's their little secret?" In truth, there's really nothing remarkable about what they do.

1. Bandelow, B., and S. Michaelis. 2015. "Epidemiology of Anxiety Disorders in the 21st Century." Dialogues in Clinical Neuroscience 17(3):327–35. doi: 10.31887/DCNS.2015.17.3/bbandelow. PMID: 26487813; PMCID: PMC4610617.

At a very simple level, they've learned to put anxiety and other unpleasant feelings and thoughts in their proper place—where they are just a *part* of life, not the *whole* of it. At a deeper level, they've learned to free themselves from the constant struggle with anxiety. They've come to find a peace of mind that persists no matter what life brings. And they don't let anxiety, fear, worry, panic, painful memories, and the like stand in the way of doing what they care deeply about.

The journal you have in your hands will help you do this too. Anxiety need not continue to cause you to suffer by putting a choke hold on you and your life. There's another way: a set of skills we'll help you learn so that you can devote more of your energies to aspects of your life that matter to you. This innovative approach, supported by solid research, will help you tip the scales back to where anxiety and fear become just a *part* of living well.

To get there, you'll first need to be brutally honest with yourself. You've probably tried many things, large and small, to keep anxiety and fear at bay. But nothing has really worked. You're still struggling with anxiety, and perhaps you've watched your life get smaller and smaller over time. That's why you picked up this book, right?

You want your life to feel big and full again. Well, consider how your current mindset may be contributing to the problem. You see, inside the "anxiety is a problem" mindset is typically a relationship with anxiety that's hostile and unkind. This tension simply feeds and strengthens anxiety. And, as anxiety grows, you'll tend to struggle with it and resist it even more—and on and on it goes in an endless cycle.

We're not going to ask you to participate in any part of that cycle in this journal. You won't find strategies that involve fighting the anxiety or fanning the flames of fear. You won't find techniques that don't work in the long run. Here, we're going help you do something new so you can get a different outcome in your life.

The most powerful antidote to this never-ending cycle is to learn how to bring acceptance, kindness, and compassion to your anxious thoughts and feelings. It may seem like a tall order now, but as you'll discover in these pages, it's resistance to what we wish we didn't feel that keeps anxiety going.

Peace of mind comes when we let go of the need to resist. Developing acceptance and compassion for the more painful parts of your inner emotional life will weaken the power of anxiety that keeps you stuck and suffering. And it'll do something else too—something that is larger and far more important than anxiety itself. It will allow you to create space to discover, or perhaps rediscover, what you want to be about in this life and where you want to go. As that space grows, you'll learn to refocus your energies on the people and experiences that matter most to you. And, as strange as it may sound now, you'll learn how to engage in your life more fully and deeply. When you do more of that, you can expect to think and feel better too.

There's a helpful Buddhist saying that the journey of a thousand miles begins with one step. Getting your hands on this journal is one step in a new direction. And working through the journal, even up to this point, is yet another step on your journey out of your anxiety and into a new life.

You'll face some challenging situations as you continue to move yourself forward. But you'll also learn, progress, and see life in a way that you may never have experienced before. Living according to your values, not just to avoid your anxiety, is something we will help you do more of, one step at a time. Through it all, the important thing is that you are taking steps, for even tiny steps will eventually take you up a mountain.

We invite you to make this journal your travel guide. It's divided into three sections—Notice, Allow, and Do—each covering a set of skills and strategies to shift your relationship with anxiety and your life. You will learn to step back and **Notice** what you feel and experience as it is, **Allow** it to be there without resistance, and **Do** more of what you really care about, even when anxiety happens.

As you work through this journal, you will create the space you need to move *with* anxiety rather than against it. It's time for you to start living the kind of life you wish you live. . . . **So let's begin.**

PART 1

Noticing

Letting Go of Anxiety Myths

You probably know quite a bit about anxiety and its disorders already from your own experience, from articles and books, from the Internet, or from conversations with family, friends, or your doctor. You may have heard that anxiety disorders are a disease, just like diabetes or cancer, or that some people inherit anxiety disorders. You may also have heard that anxiety disorders can be treated with herbal remedies or by changing your diet. Others may have told you that anxiety disorders are caused by your brain's neurochemicals run amok, so you absolutely need medications to repair chemical imbalances within your faulty brain. Or perhaps you've heard that learning better ways to manage and control your thoughts and feelings is a way out of your anxiety.

The message behind many of these claims is that it's abnormal to experience intense fear and anxiety. Which means that if you are dealing with fear and anxiety, then something's wrong with you. You might even think that you are weak, broken, or on the verge of going crazy. But nothing could be further from the truth.

These common beliefs about anxiety are even accepted by some mental health professionals. Yet none of them are true; each is a myth or, at best, a half-truth. In reality, these false beliefs keep you stuck in old patterns that don't work. They leave you wanting, waiting, and struggling to get a foothold. They feed an erroneous belief that everyone else around you just glides through life happy and carefree. This isn't so. So let's take a look at the myths and reveal them for what they are.

Myth: Anxiety Is Inherited and I Can't Get Rid of It

Take a moment to inhale three deep breaths. Now think for a moment about all of the things you know about anxiety.

I know that...

Anxiety feels like _____

_____

Anxiety looks like _____

_____

Anxiety can be _____

_____

Anxiety cannot be _____

_____

Anxiety is _____

_____

Think for a moment about what you just wrote. How is your experience of anxiety similar to what you know about anxiety?

_____

_____

_____

_____

_____

_____

_____

How is it different?

> Anxiety problems aren't biological or hereditary; you're not simply stuck with them. Your brain and body are constantly changing depending on what you do. There's always room to grow and become the person you wish to be in this life.

_____

_____

_____

_____

_____

_____

_____

_____

Myth: Anxiety Makes Me Abnormal

One of the main reasons people seek help for anxiety is that they don't like how they think or feel. Does that resonate with you? Use the space below to reflect on how anxiety makes you feel. Does it seem overwhelming? Are painful memories too much to bear? Do you have thoughts and worries that feel paralyzing or next to impossible to turn off? Be as descriptive as possible.

Do you sometimes feel as if your anxiety is abnormal or that it has somehow wired you differently than others?

Circle one.   **YES**   NO

Do you see anxiety as your enemy?

Circle one.   **YES**   NO

Myth: Anxiety Is a Sign of Weakness

Perhaps you're having a hard time believing that other people have anxiety too. For a moment, bring to mind some individuals in your life who seem very well put together. They are making it, doing things that you'd like to do. They are generally always happy and content when you see them. They seem to manage any of life's difficulties with ease because they're strong.

> Intense anxiety doesn't make anxiety a problem. Many people experience intense anxiety in their daily lives and continue to follow through on what's important to them. Remember that anxiety is just one vital part of you.

Now try to see the world through their eyes, from birth up to where they are right now. Imagine everything this person might've experienced, not just the perfect stuff you see from the outside. Write down ways that they may have struggled behind the "perfect" life you see.

_____

_____

_____

_____

Anxiety isn't a sign of weakness, personality defect, poor character, laziness, or lack of motivation. Anyone can get stuck or go off track because of emotional or psychological pain. All human beings will face obstacles, problems, and pain. This truth is part of the human condition.

Myth: Ridding Myself of Anxiety Will Make My Life Better

You have surely imagined what life might be like if you were able to rid yourself of anxiety. So let's use that energy to brainstorm what your life would be like if you were one of the "perfect" people you admire. Go ahead and write it all down. Don't be shy about it. A bit of dreaming is more than welcome.

Now reread what you just wrote. Does anything stand out? We're willing to bet that underlying the description of your anxiety-free life is a common message that most of us buy into:

In order to live better, I must first think and feel better. And once I start thinking and feeling better, my life will improve for the better.

This is a trap. Of all the anxiety myths, this one is the most damaging. It's fueled by social rules and expectations, or what we call the *culture of feel-goodism*. These rules frame emotional and physical pain as barriers to a life lived well. They lead you to believe that if you experience emotional pain, it's a problem, and you need to fix that problem to be happy. This belief pulls many people into a struggle with genuine aspects of what they think and feel.

The bait for the trap is the emotional and psychological pain you experience with anxiety, panic, worries, unwanted thoughts, or memories. In your mind, this pain isn't just pain. It's *bad* pain. Your mind has judged it as unacceptable and labeled it a barrier to being able to do what you care about. So, when anxiety pain shows up, you go after it to weaken it or drive it away. You do this or that to prevent that *bad* pain from showing up in the future, yet it always returns. And on and on the battle goes.

One Myth I Have Is…

You may have an anxiety myth we didn't cover. If so, what is it?

_____

_____

_____

Now try rebutting your myth. Can you place yourself on the other side of it? Try to notice any cracks in its armor. Are there any assumptions in the myth that don't hold true? Write these down.

_____

_____

_____

_____

_____

_____

_____

_____

_____

_____

Now take a second to think back on all your reflections about myths. Which myth holds the most sway? Circle that.

- Anxiety is inherited and I cannot get rid of it.

- Anxiety makes me abnormal.

- Anxiety is a sign of weakness.

- Ridding myself of anxiety will make my life better.

- Having anxiety is a problem.

My myth: _____

_____

_____

Go further and ask yourself, *Is holding on to any myth helpful to my lived experience? Or is it limiting for me?*

_____

_____

_____

_____

_____

_____

_____

_____

_____

_____

_____

_____

Noticing Anxiety for What It Is

Now that you've broken free of some unhelpful anxious myths, it is important to begin noticing anxiety for what it really is: a bunch of thoughts that tangle you up, physical sensations in your body, feelings, and urges to act or react. For the next three days, jot down any thoughts, worries, emotional experiences, or memories that particularly upset you. For each one, describe events or experiences that tend to go along with it. The key practice here is simply to notice the components of your anxiety experience.

Date: _____

What I experienced:

My anxiety
level was:

10
9
8
7
6
5
4
3
2
1
0

What went along with it:

1.

2.

3.

4.

5.

Date: _____

What I experienced:

My anxiety level was:

10
9
8
7
6
5
4
3
2
1
0

What went along with it:

1.

2.

3.

4.

5.

Date: _____

What I experienced:

My anxiety
level was:

10
9
8
7
6
5
4
3
2
1
0

What went along with it:

1.

2.

3.

4.

5.

Now that you've practiced noticing for a few days, how did it go? What did you discover about the anxiety you're experiencing? Did your anxiety levels change? If so, what did you notice that is new or different?

_____

_____

_____

_____

_____

_____

What anxiety myths have you bought into? How will you let go of the myths?

_____

_____

_____

_____

_____

_____

What needs to happen now is for you to take stock. What have you and your life become because of your battles with anxiety? Now is the time for you to take a stand and decide that you no longer want to be about that. This is a choice only you can make—but you *can* make it.

Facing the Costs

What impact has anxiety had on your relationships? Have friendships changed or been lost? Have family members been alienated? Do loved ones avoid you, or do you avoid them? Maybe you've even lost a marriage or romantic relationship—or missed out on new connections—due to worry, anxiety, or fear. Go slow and be honest with yourself as you write.

What has struggling with anxiety done to your career? Have you ever quit or been fired from a job because of attempts to get a handle on your anxiety or fear? Have you faced other consequences, such as being late to work, avoiding tasks because anxious feelings might show up, being unwilling to travel, or passing up job opportunities?

Now, consider the effects of managing your worry, anxiety, and fear on your health. Circle the answer that best describes your habits.

Do you tend to get sick often?	YES	NO
Do you have difficulties falling asleep or staying asleep?	YES	NO
Do you sometimes ruminate or stew over anxiety or worry to the point of feeling sick or keyed up?	YES	NO
Do you avoid taking care of your health because of your anxiety (for example, avoid going to the doctor, having tests done, visiting a dentist)?	YES	NO
Do you avoid exercise because of it?	YES	NO
Has your eating or diet changed (for example, you overeat, undereat, make poor food choices)?	YES	NO
Do you turn to drugs or alcohol to cope?	YES	NO
Have you spent quite a bit of time in the doctor's office or emergency room?	YES	NO

How has managing your anxiety affected your energy?

Are you constantly reliving painful moments from your past or feeling trapped in the doom and gloom your mind feeds you about the future?   YES   NO

Do you spend needless time checking or performing rituals to feel more comfortable or to ward off catastrophe?   YES   NO

Have your attempts to manage anxiety left you feeling discouraged, fatigued, frustrated, or worn out?   YES   NO

When you get in touch with the costs of anxiety, you can clearly see what doesn't serve you. But unless you're willing to face that reality, you'll continue to do what you've always done.

When you have tried to get a handle on anxiety, what has it cost you emotionally? Do you feel sad or depressed about having anxiety? Maybe you tend to be on edge, exploding in anger. Maybe you carry regrets and guilt because of what you've done or failed to do. Maybe you even feel like life's passing you by... If so, describe your feelings.

_____

_____

_____

_____

_____

_____

_____

_____

_____

How much money have you spent on managing your anxiety? Consider money you've spent on psychotherapy. How about the cost of medications, doctor visits, anxiety books, audio or video recordings, or seminars? See if you can come up with a reasonable estimate of these monetary costs. Include costs due to disability, lost wages, missing out on important or enjoyable events (for example, concerts, plane trips, dinners out), and missed work.

How have your efforts to control anxiety limited your ability to do what you enjoy and want to do? Try to complete the following sentence: Anxiety keeps me from...

_____

_____

_____

_____

_____

_____

_____

_____

_____

_____

_____

This may seem an exhaustive, even painful exercise. But seeing what anxiety keeps you from is a "noticing" practice. This noticing is essential for you to pry apart the hold that anxiety has. It's also a practice that takes time to get good at.

For the next few days, use this journal to record more about the situations in which you're anxious.

Date: _____

Describe the situation or event that triggered your anxiety, panic, concerns, or worries.

_____

_____

_____

_____

_____

_____

Describe your anxiety, bodily sensations, thoughts, concerns, or worries.

_____

_____

_____

_____

_____

_____

_____

_____

What did you do to manage your anxiety?

_____

_____

_____

_____

_____

_____

How did your efforts to control or reduce your anxiety work for you? Circle one.

ANXIETY WENT AWAY | LITTLE TO NO EFFECT | ANXIETY GOT WORSE

Were there consequences or costs to these coping strategies? Did they limit your ability to do what you enjoy or want to do?

_____

_____

_____

_____

_____

_____

Date: _____

Describe the situation or event that triggered your anxiety, panic, concerns, or worries.

_____

_____

_____

_____

_____

Describe your anxiety, bodily sensations, thoughts, concerns, or worries.

_____

_____

_____

_____

_____

_____

_____

_____

What did you do to manage your anxiety?

_____

_____

_____

_____

_____

_____

How did your efforts to control or reduce your anxiety work for you? Circle one.

ANXIETY WENT AWAY | LITTLE TO NO EFFECT | ANXIETY GOT WORSE

Were there consequences or costs to these coping strategies? Did they limit your ability to do what you enjoy or want to do?

_____

_____

_____

_____

_____

_____

_____

Date: _____

Describe the situation or event that triggered your anxiety, panic, concerns, or worries.

_____

_____

_____

_____

_____

Describe your anxiety, bodily sensations, thoughts, concerns, or worries.

_____

_____

_____

_____

_____

_____

What did you do to manage your anxiety?

_____

_____

_____

_____

_____

_____

How did your efforts to control or reduce your anxiety work for you? Circle one.

ANXIETY WENT AWAY | LITTLE TO NO EFFECT | ANXIETY GOT WORSE

Were there consequences or costs to these coping strategies? Did they limit your ability to do what you enjoy or want to do?

_____

_____

_____

_____

_____

_____

_____

Now that you've spent a few days noticing your experiences with anxiety, what does your heart or gut tell you about your struggle with anxiety? What do your experiences tell you about your response to anxious situations? Take a moment to take stock.

_____

_____

_____

_____

_____

_____

_____

_____

_____

_____

> Everything you've done to avoid and resist anxiety has cost you. Avoidance shrinks your life, and resistance makes anxiety grow. The way out of the anxiety trap is to decide that you will no longer resist and avoid your own experience.

Re-Centering Yourself

Right now, take a moment to check in with yourself. Take a couple of gentle breaths: in...and out...in...and out. Notice the sound and feel of your own breath as you breathe in...and out.

Now turn your attention to being just where you are. Just being. There's nothing to do but be in this moment, resting in an awareness of your breath as you breathe in...and out.

When you're ready, expand your awareness just a bit and get in touch with why you're here, writing in this journal. Notice the investment you're making in your life. Many other people, just like you, are also making similar investments in their own lives. And what you're doing in this moment is an act of courage, integrity, and self-love. This courageous act of yours connects you with many other people from all walks of life who are doing the same.

Notice any doubts, reservations, fears, and worries. You don't need to make them go away or work on them. With each breath, imagine that you are creating more and more space for them—and more space for you to be you, right here where you are, at peace with what is.

Gently ask yourself, *Am I willing to learn how to change my relationship with my anxious mind and body, and allow them to be there as just another part of me? Can I do this instead of fighting them, which hasn't really worked? Are the things I really want to do and be in this life important enough for me to be willing to do this?*

Then, when you are ready, gradually widen your attention to take in the sounds around you and slowly open your eyes.

Learning to Be Here Now

Your thoughts, feelings, sensations, and memories are all parts of your internal experience. Your judgmental mind can readily turn anything that is normally fluid and flexible—like your internal experience—into something hard and heavy that's bullying you around and ruining your life. *Mindful allowing* is a stance toward life that can break you out of this cycle.

When you practice mindful allowing, you're watching your experience without judging it, feeling the pain without drowning in it, and honoring the hurt without becoming it. It isn't a feeling or an attitude. It is a choice to open up and be with whatever is happening anyway.

With this type of allowing, you're actively doing something new—often something that is the opposite of what you've been doing. You are choosing to open and be with what is, just as it is. Or you're choosing to stay when you used to run away in the past.

Soften when your tendency is to harden. Expand when you'd rather contract. Lean into life when your impulse is to turn away. Nurture your capacity for gentleness, kindness, and compassion.

Sharpening Your Skill at Noticing

Let's try another exercise to help you with awareness. Close your eyes and imagine a long-stemmed rose, freshly cut after a gentle rain, hovering in front of you.

Notice all the details: the textures, smell, shapes, and colors.

Notice the light and shadows, the dew drops, and the stem. In your mind, simply notice the qualities of the rose and your experience of it. Now write about it carefully in detail.

Now pause for a second. As you did this exercise, did your mind throw in judgments or evaluations of the rose? If so, what were they?

_____

_____

_____

_____

_____

_____

_____

_____

You might have thought, _How beautiful_, or _It smells really nice_. Your mind could have readily come up with more negative evaluations too, like, _That's an ugly rose, This exercise sucks_, or _What a stupid rose_.

Notice though that your evaluations don't change the rose one bit—the rose is a rose regardless of what your mind calls it. Notice also that your evaluations of the rose aren't the rose. The rose won't change because your mind calls it this or that.

Mindful allowing is a powerful way to notice when you're caught up in evaluations of your experience more than in the raw experience itself. Allowing calls you to open up to life just as it is.

Feel free to use the rest of the page to draw that rose.

When you meet the hardness of your judgmental mind
with softness, you weaken its power. Anxieties, hurts,
fears, shame, anger, or remorse—they all lose their power.
You can live life free of the suffering with anxiety.

Mindful Allowing Meditation

Let's try applying mindful allowing to your experience of anxiety.

- Set a timer for ten minutes.

- Get in a comfortable position in your chair.

- Allow your eyes to close gently.

- Take a few moments to get in touch with the movement of your breath. Slowly bring your attention to the gentle rising and falling of your breath in your chest and belly. Like ocean waves coming in and out, your breath is always there.

- There's no need to control your breathing. Simply let the breath breathe itself. As best you can, bring an attitude of generous allowing and gentle acceptance to your experience, just as it is.

- As you continue breathing, your mind will wander away from the breath to other concerns, thoughts, worries, images, bodily sensations, planning, or daydreams, or it may just drift along. This is what minds do much of the time. When you notice that your mind has wandered, just acknowledge that awareness of your experience.

- Then, gently, and with kindness, come back to the breath. If you become aware of feelings, tension, or other intense physical sensations, just notice them, acknowledge their presence, and see if you can make space for them.

- Name them if you like.

Then, gently, and with kindness, come back to the breath.

You may notice sensations in your body, then come back to the breath.

You may notice your mind coming up with evaluations such as "dangerous" or "getting worse," or "bored." Then come back to the breath.

You may also notice thoughts about the sensations and thoughts about the thoughts. If that happens, notice those thoughts as thoughts, and return to the breath and the present moment, just as it is.

Remind yourself that you're getting better at noticing and being with all that is you, as it is, in this moment. This is the mindful allowing practice.

Then, when you're ready, gradually widen your attention to take in the sounds around you...and slowly open your eyes.

Allowing is counterintuitive. But if you learn to allow anxiety, rather than trying to make it go away, you'll reclaim the attention and energy you need to do the things you want to do.

Control Is the Real Problem

Now let's try another exercise: make yourself feel happy. Go ahead and try. Just make yourself as happy as you know how to be. Really work at it. Then write about your attempt.

_____

_____

_____

_____

_____

_____

_____

_____

_____

_____

Were you successful?	YES	NO
Did you need to think about a happy memory or visualize something entertaining?	YES	NO

If you needed to conjure up a memory of a beautiful experience from your past, visualize something you like, or thought of an event you are looking forward to, you needed something to respond to, to feel happy. Notice how you couldn't just flip a switch and be super happy for the sake of it, rather than as a response to something.

Now try to make yourself feel really anxious or afraid. Do it without thinking about something really scary or painful. We want you to try really hard to just turn on the anxiety switch. Can you do it? Jot down your thoughts.

If you're still not convinced about how impossible this really is, then try to:

- Make yourself fall madly in love—meaning genuine, deeply felt love—with the first new person you see.
- Make your left leg numb, so numb in fact that if it was pricked with a sharp needle you wouldn't feel a thing.

Impossible, right? The simple lesson here is this: we can't control internal experience. We can't control happy and joyful existence any more than we can unwanted and painful aspects of our private worlds. Trying to control what you cannot control isn't a solution. It's the *problem*.

This means it's important to start letting go of the anxiety-management agenda, so you can get on with your *life*-management agenda—and do so feeling calm, open, energized, and capable.

It may not always feel like it, but you can *choose* the kind of relationship you wish to have with your emotional life, just as you do with other people.

Renegotiating Your Relationship with Anxiety

Go ahead and think of your anxiety as a person. Give it a name. Imagine how it looks, how it dresses, its voice, personality, age, gender, and how it speaks to you.

Name: _____

_____

_____

_____

_____

_____

_____

_____

_____

_____

_____

Once you have this character clearly in your mind, imagine that it shows up on your doorstep one day uninvited. What does it tell you? How would you respond?

_____

_____

_____

_____

_____

_____

_____

_____

_____

_____

_____

Does this character give you useful advice as far as your life is concerned?   YES   NO

You might be ambivalent. Maybe some part of you wants to just slam the door in your anxiety's face. Of course, that wouldn't be something you'd do in a healthy relationship with another person in your life. This is where things need to change. The choice here is to practice a more inviting and welcoming relationship with your anxiety. But this doesn't mean you have to listen to this character's advice and always do what it tells you to do.

Even an impulse to act is a feeling. But the action is not inevitable. There's a split second between every impulse and every action. In this gap, you can pause, pivot, and decide what you're going to do and how you're going to respond.

When your anxiety shows up,

you can acknowledge its presence,

allow it to be there,

and make room for something new.

To help you get a sense of this, spend a few more days this week noticing situations where your anxiety character shows up. Afterward, write about them.

Date: _____

What was my internal experience (my thoughts, feelings, sensations)?

_____

_____

_____

_____

_____

_____

What was my impulse (my anxiety coping actions)?

_____

_____

_____

_____

What were the consequences of my response? What did I lose or miss out on?

_____

_____

_____

_____

How would I describe the tone of my relationship with my anxiety character in that moment (for example, uncaring, unloving, unkind, loving, friendly, caring, supportive, kind, compassionate)?

_____

_____

_____

_____

Now brainstorm some life-affirming alternative actions and write them down.

_____

_____

_____

_____

_____

_____

_____

_____

MORE ➤

What would the consequences of these new responses have been? What would I have gained in my life?

_____

_____

_____

_____

_____

_____

What would the tone of my relationship with my anxiety have been had I chosen more life-affirming actions (for example, loving, friendly, caring, supportive, kind, compassionate)?

_____

_____

_____

_____

_____

_____

_____

Date: _____

What was my internal experience (my thoughts, feelings, sensations)?

_____

_____

_____

_____

_____

_____

What was my impulse (my anxiety coping actions)?

_____

_____

_____

_____

What were the consequences of my response? What did I lose or miss out on?

_____

_____

_____

_____

MORE

How would I describe the tone of my relationship with my anxiety character in that moment (for example, uncaring, unloving, unkind, loving, friendly, caring, supportive, kind, compassionate)?

_____

_____

_____

_____

_____

Now brainstorm some life-affirming alternative actions and write them down.

_____

_____

_____

_____

_____

_____

_____

_____

_____

What would the consequences of these new responses have been? What would I have gained in my life?

_____

_____

_____

_____

_____

_____

What would the tone of my relationship with my anxiety have been had I chosen more life-affirming actions (for example, loving, friendly, caring, supportive, kind, compassionate)?

_____

_____

_____

_____

_____

_____

Date: _____

What was my internal experience (my thoughts, feelings, sensations)?

_____

_____

_____

_____

_____

_____

What was my impulse (my anxiety coping actions)?

_____

_____

_____

_____

What were the consequences of my response? What did I lose or miss out on?

_____

_____

_____

_____

How would I describe the tone of my relationship with my anxiety character in that moment (for example, uncaring, unloving, unkind, loving, friendly, caring, supportive, kind, compassionate)?

_____

_____

_____

_____

Now brainstorm some life-affirming alternative actions and write them down.

_____

_____

_____

_____

_____

What would the consequences of these new responses have been? What would I have gained in my life?

_____

_____

_____

_____

MORE

What would the tone of my relationship with my anxiety have been had I chosen more life-affirming actions (for example, loving, friendly, caring, supportive, kind, compassionate)?

_____

_____

_____

_____

_____

_____

No matter how powerful the anxiety feelings and impulses to act are, you do have control and choices in this moment.

Responsibility means you're able to respond, or *response-able*. You don't have responsibility for anxiety showing up—that's out of your control. But you are response-able for how you respond and what you decide to do when it's there.

Choices, Actions, Destiny

So what is your destiny? What determines what your life will become? The answer is simple: it's the cumulative effect of your choices and your actions. This is the prize!

This doesn't mean that the outcome of your choices and actions will always be what you want. Many events in life, both good and bad, happen outside of your control. And nobody knows what the future will hold. What most people hope for is that the cumulative effect of their choices and actions will yield a sense of a life well lived. Everything you do from here on out adds up to that.

CHOICE + ACTIONS = YOUR DESTINY.

What destiny do you think your anxiety's led you toward so far?

_____

_____

_____

_____

_____

_____

_____

What destiny would you *want* to be led toward?

As you'll discover, the more open you are to what arises in your internal experience, the more the choices you make and the actions you take will align with the destiny you aspire toward.

Willingness

It is certainly difficult to do something we don't want to do. But our goal here is to foster your willingness to take your emotions with you while you act in the service of your goals and dreams. This is a choice, not a feeling. It is also a leap of faith with each step you take.

"I'll try" is often what we say in situations like this: *Next time I'm anxious, I'll really try to be willing and not do what I usually do.* But willingness isn't about *trying* to do something. It's about doing it. And it's about doing it without focusing on the outcome. After all, even if you're 100 percent willing, you may not always get what you want.

And that's okay. Some things in life *require* persistence: you need to do them over and over before you accomplish your goal. And getting attached to failure isn't any more helpful than getting attached to anxiety.

So are you willing to go out with your hands and feet and take your anxiety with you? Remember, willingness is neither a feeling nor a thought. Willingness is simply a choice and a commitment to have what you already have. This frees you up to go where you want to go.

On the next page, you'll find a contract you can sign to make your commitment to moving toward the things you value, taking your anxiety with you.

I, _____, am willing to

take my anxiety with me as I use my hands

and feet to move myself in the directions I

want my life to take.

Signature: _____

Date: _____

You are much more than your worries, anxieties, and fears.

Holding Anxiety Kindly

Are you ready to try another exercise? Take a second to look at your hands. Maybe one's helping hold this book open, and the other's holding a pencil or pen near this page. Become aware that those very hands have been used by you in many, many ways. They have been used for work, for love, to touch and be touched, to heal, to share kindness...

Reflect on the good things your hands have helped you do. Write them down.

Now take both of your hands and cup them to make the shape of a bowl, palms facing up. Allow them to rest softly in your lap. Notice the quality of those hands and the shape they are in. They are open and ready to hold something.

And from that place of goodness, see if you can allow, even if just for a moment, a small, tiny piece of your anxiety concerns to settle there. Like a feather floating down, imagine that piece of your anxiety gently coming to rest in the middle of your kind and loving hands.

This piece of your anxiety is now resting within the goodness of your hands. What is it like to hold a piece of your anxiety and yourself this way? Simply notice, breathe, and sense the warmth and goodness of your hands. There's nothing else to do here.

You, the Observer
of Your Life

Recall that your thoughts and feelings—all of them—are a part of you. But they are not *you*.

This is a very important distinction. Anxiety and fear are emotions you experience periodically. They may explode into your awareness...and after a while, they recede. You—the person who experiences and observes your life—remain. Like every other thought or emotion, your anxiety has its moment on the stage, then slips into the wings. The only permanent, immutable thing is you—the audience—the observer of your life.

When you were born, you were just two eyes looking out onto the world—a *you-perspective* looking out on the world—without any experience of that world. You were much like an empty vessel. And then quickly, you started to collect experiences. You tasted, touched, felt, began to speak, talked about your past, your self, your future. Your vessel was no longer empty. It started to fill. And it'll continue to fill as long as you're alive.

Right now, you might spend a lot of time with the stuff you have collected so far. Maybe you identify with it. Maybe you're trying to get rid of some of it, to cover up things that you don't like very much, or to rearrange things so that your load is easier to carry.

But we'd like to ask you: What's the one constant that's been with you throughout your life until now? Is it the experiences you collected? Or is it that vessel—that pristine *you*—that holds it all?

That is the you that was there at the moment you came into this world, before the hardship and pain, before the losses and joys, before the trauma, and before anxiety was a problem. That vessel is the real you—the holder and observer of your life—your safe refuge. It is there always. And it never changes even though everything else in your body and around you is always changing.

And with practice you can learn to sense it more clearly and let it help and guide you.

As a result of years of struggling with your anxiety, you may have focused too much on what is seemingly wrong with you. So much so, in fact, that you've lost sight of other important aspects of yourself and your life. So in this entry, think about key aspects of yourself and your life that have nothing to do with your anxiety. How would you describe yourself?

I am _____

_____

I am a person who _____

_____

I am not someone who _____

_____

I really like _____

_____

I do not like _____

_____

My most important relationship is _____

_____

I also describe myself in this way: _____

_____

_____

_____

_____

_____

The truth is that all of these descriptions—even the most detailed ones—are ultimately incomplete and inadequate. Your mind uses what you've collected so far in the vessel that is your being to describe you and to tell stories about you and your life; if you continued long enough, you would run out of words to describe who you are.

And that's the point. The problem is not that we don't have enough or the right words to describe ourselves. The problem is that language can never capture ourselves fully. This is because there is an aspect of our selves—our core and essence—that goes beyond words and the stuff we've collected in our vessels.

Before you move on, take a couple of gentle breaths—in...and out...in...and out.

Now imagine you're watching yourself in a mirror.

Describe what you see: _____

_____

_____

_____

_____

_____

_____

_____

The eyes looking back at you now are the very same eyes that were there on your first day of school. Can you still remember that day? What did you see with your eyes then? And what was happening inside of you that day? Do you notice any emotions you were having...any thoughts?

_____

_____

_____

_____

_____

_____

_____

As you observe these things in your past, we'd like you to also notice that there was a part of you noticing them. A part of you observed those sensations... those sounds...thoughts...and feelings. And that part of you we will call the "observer you." There is a person inside you, behind your eyes, who is aware of what is happening right now. And it is the same person you've been all your life. How do you see this "observer you"?

Now we'd like you to remember the day you met a first girlfriend or boyfriend. Or, if your memory of that event is too faint, then remember the day you met a recent partner or friend. Remember all the things that were happening then... Recall the sights...the sounds...the smells...your feelings...your thoughts...

_____

_____

_____

_____

_____

_____

_____

_____

_____

Now think about this: the you who is here now is the same you that was there then. Yes, your feelings, thoughts, and sensations are constantly changing. But no matter what, there is a you there behind your eyes who is not changing but simply observing how you move through life.

See if you can take advantage of this distinction to let go of your worries, anxieties, and fears just a little bit. You can be secure in the knowledge that you have been you through it all, and that you need not be so invested in your emotional weather as a measure of your life. You can be the sky in which weather arises—and passes—all on its own.

Being the Sky

Over the next few days, as you encounter anxious moments in daily life, try to track what *your mind* does from the perspective of *your observing self*. See if it helps you figure out what you could do instead, as if you are the sky, and not the weather, as if you are the vessel, not the stuff inside your vessel.

Date: _____

Describe your anxious moment.

_____

_____

_____

_____

What am I feeling besides anxiety, panic, fear, or tension?

_____

_____

_____

_____

What am I saying to myself? What "good" or "bad" or "right" or "wrong" thoughts am I experiencing? Are these my thoughts, the stories my mind creates, or ideas from someone else (a parent, a friend, society)?

_____

_____

_____

_____

What am I driven to do now? Where's the urge to avoid discomfort trying to take me?

What do I want to be about right now? What do I want my life to be about right now?

Date: _____

Describe your anxious moment.

_____

_____

_____

_____

What am I feeling besides anxiety, panic, fear, or tension?

_____

_____

_____

_____

What am I saying to myself? What "good" or "bad" or "right" or "wrong" thoughts am I experiencing? Are these my thoughts, the stories my mind creates, or ideas from someone else (a parent, a friend, society)?

_____

_____

_____

_____

What am I driven to do now? Where's the urge to avoid discomfort trying to take me?

_____

_____

_____

_____

_____

_____

What do I want to be about right now? What do I want my life to be about right now?

_____

_____

_____

_____

_____

_____

Date: ....

Describe your anxious moment.

_____

_____

_____

_____

What am I feeling besides anxiety, panic, fear, or tension?

_____

_____

_____

_____

What am I saying to myself? What "good" or "bad" or "right" or "wrong" thoughts am I experiencing? Are these my thoughts, the stories my mind creates, or ideas from someone else (a parent, a friend, society)?

_____

_____

_____

_____

What am I driven to do now? Where's the urge to avoid discomfort trying to take me?

_____

_____

_____

_____

_____

_____

What do I want to be about right now? What do I want my life to be about right now?

_____

_____

_____

_____

_____

_____

Your mind may not always be your best friend,
but your true self is.

"I Am"

Becoming a good observer is important for anyone struggling with anxiety. Why? Because it helps you to gain a helpful perspective and experience. Notice and write down what happens inside of you when you read the next four statements.

I am an anxious person.

_____

_____

_____

_____

I am too shy.

_____

_____

_____

_____

I am not good enough.

_____

_____

_____

_____

_____

_____

I am never going to make it.

_____

_____

_____

_____

_____

_____

Did you notice how your mind almost immediately started to "work on" these statements, perhaps agreeing or disagreeing with them, rephrasing or qualifying them, making them stronger, toning them down, defending them with reasons and justifications, and so on?

Now think about some troubling descriptions of yourself that your mind offers up to you regularly. What does your mind tell you about who you "are"? What does your mind tell you that you "are not"?

I am:

I am:

I am:

I am:

I am not:

I am not:

I am not:

I am not:

Now think about how it might feel to answer the question *Who am I really?* with a simple, disarming *I am*. No qualifications! No arguments, explanations, justifications, or anything else. Just a simple statement of being. It's the simplest and easiest way to drop all those evaluative self-statements your mind constantly dishes out to you—once and for all, anytime. *I am who I am!* So try it out.

I am.

PART 2

Allowing

Words Are Just Words

Your mind can be your greatest friend and your worst enemy. It all depends on what you do with it. There's nothing packed between your ears that can do you harm. Thoughts are just thoughts, ethereal, without form or substance. Things that you might imagine or visualize in your mind are like that too. They can seem quite real, but when you look at them, you'll find that there really isn't much to them at all.

Let's start with the word "spider." What does this creature look like in your mind? Can you see it crawling? You may even feel a little anxious or disgusted if spiders scare you in real life. Write out everything that comes to mind when you see the word "spider"—or draw it, if you prefer.

Now pull out your phone and open the clock app, or sit somewhere near a clock with a second hand. You are going to use it to keep time for forty seconds. Now read the following as fast as you can:

spider spider spider spider spider spider spider spider spider spider spider spider
spider spider spider spider spider spider spider spider spider spider spider spider
spider spider spider spider spider spider spider spider spider

spider spider spider spider spider spider

spider spider spider spider spider

spider spider spider spider

spider spider spider

What happened to the meaning of "spider" after forty seconds? Did it still make you feel creepy (if you did feel creepy)? Did it continue to summon the image of the spider? Did the words start running together into strange sounds? Or did spider change in some way? Use the space below for your reflections—or draw the new version, if you like.

Now let's try the exercise with an anxious-type word. Pick a word that reminds you of your anxiety, like "worry," "panic," "anxiousness," "aloneness," "space," "airplane," "sadness," "death," "dirtiness," "sickness," "heights," "crashes," or "crowdedness."

My anxiety word is _____.

What comes to mind when you see this word? Is it a memory, or a feeling? Describe it as best as you can, in words or by drawing.

Now, using a clock again, set a timer for forty seconds. Then use the space below to see how many times you can write down the word. Do it as fast as humanly possible.

How do you feel now that you've written this anxious word so many times? Does it still sound as believable? Can you see how it's also just a word, a sound with no meaning or truth? Take a moment to jot down what is showing up for you.

_____

_____

_____

_____

_____

_____

_____

_____

This is a useful exercise for helping you see that the products of your judgmental mind can create an illusion of monsters that are not monsters at all.

You can create even more space from anxious thoughts by saying the thought out loud and *slowly*, like "woooooorrrrrryyyy," "stuuuuupid," or "unreeeeeal." Or say it in another voice—as a child or an old person, as Minnie Mouse or Donald Duck, as someone intoxicated, or as a grumpy person. Or you can put your thought to music. Take the thought and sing it to yourself. Put it to the melody of a favorite holiday tune, children's song, or whatever song you'd like. See what happens to the thought as you manipulate it in this way.

The Judgmental Mind

Think of a key unsettling message your mind feeds you about you and your life before, during, or after you're anxious or afraid. Now think what this mind of yours would be like if it were a person you just met.

What kind of person are you dealing with here? Maybe it's the same character you imagined your anxiety being before, or maybe it's a different one. Either way, is this a caring, loving person? Is this someone you'd like to spend time with? Would you want to be friends or have this person over for dinner? Explain.

Now think about what your mind is saying to you. Is it helpful? Maybe there's a seed of wisdom in what your mind has said, or the intention behind it, that you want to listen to. Or maybe you want to just let this particular thought or judgment go. What do you feel as you think about what your mind's giving you— and what action do you want to take?

Your mind can be your worst enemy and your greatest friend. The way to tell the difference is by noticing what your mind is telling you, and then asking yourself if your mind is being helpful or not. If the thoughts are unhelpful, then notice them, allow them to come and go, and focus on what you want to do with your time and energy.

Confronting Fear Feelings

The next time you have an experience of anxiety, come back to this spot in the journal. Write down a few of the thoughts and troublesome or disturbing images you are struggling with. Things like, *I felt sick to my stomach, and my heart was pounding.* Or *My hands were shaking, I was disoriented, and nobody understood me.*

Read over your list. It's okay if you don't like it or if the memory of what you experienced makes you uncomfortable. Willingness, as you're learning to practice it, is not about liking it.

Are you open to allowing it—to having that image and the discomfort that goes along with it, without doing anything about it?

_____

_____

_____

_____

Next, get settled in. Pick one thing from your list. Write it here.

_____

_____

Read out loud to yourself five times the words you wrote down above. If you start to feel uncomfortable, focus on your breath.

Now rewrite this image in the spaces below, three times:

I am having the image of _____

_____

I am having the image of _____

_____

I am having the image of _____

_____

Be patient and take your time. And bring kindness and compassion to the image, as if you were holding something that you care about deeply.

As you do, notice that this image, and whatever might be arising as you contemplate it, are just thoughts and images. It's as though you're driving a bus, and everything you're thinking and feeling—every image and sensation—is just a passenger with you on that bus. And you, not they, control the gas pedal, brake, and steering wheel. You, not they, control what you do.

Practicing compassion with your anxious mind is a powerful way to separate yourself from all this activity. It's just your mind doing what minds do. Knowing this gives you clarity and freedom to make more vital choices and take more vital actions.

If Anxiety Were an Itch...

Thoughts and feelings of panic and anxiety are unpleasant, intense, overwhelming at times, and even terrifying. But they're not the real enemy. The real enemy is rigid avoidance of fear and anxiety.

If your anxiety were an itch, how would you scratch it? What do you typically do when anxiety and fear shows up?

_____

_____

_____

_____

What kinds of things has your anxiety told you *not* to do?

_____

_____

_____

_____

_____

_____

Thinking back on those times you listened to your anxiety and chose *not* to do something, were you less anxious in that moment? Did this strategy work?

_____

_____

_____

What about a day later? Did it still work?

_____

_____

_____

What about a week later?

_____

_____

_____

Often, we discover that doing what anxiety tells us may help us feel less anxious in the moment. But inevitably, anxiety comes back. And struggling with it, rather than allowing it, comes with costs. How much longer are you willing to pay those costs?

And what if relief from the anxiety itch were available to you right now—if you just stopped scratching it?

Dropping the Struggle

Controlling anxiety doesn't work in the same way that control works in other areas of life. No matter how hard you've tried, no strategy to manage anxiety has helped long term. On top of that, the costs of the struggle are still there. So what can you do instead?

You could give up the struggle with anxiety—and surrender.

What has your struggle with anxiety been like? Seriously, what have you tried? How has your experience been?

_____

_____

_____

_____

_____

_____

_____

How has the ongoing battle with anxiety felt? How have your energy levels been? Have you felt at any point that you were close to being free of anxiety? Or has the effort been exhausting?

How has your struggle with anxiety kept you stuck in the same place with nowhere to go?

What would it mean to you to regain your freedom?

_____

_____

_____

_____

_____

_____

_____

It may seem like you've been fighting a tug-of-war with a team of anxiety monsters pulling at one end of the rope and you pulling at the other end. Yet no matter how hard you've pulled, they've always come back stronger, pulling harder.

Here's another option: you don't need to win this fight. What would happen if you decided to drop the rope and stop fighting?

_____

_____

_____

_____

_____

_____

_____

_____

_____

_____

_____

_____

_____

_____

_____

Dropping the rope and ending the struggle against
your anxiety creates an opening and room to do
something else in your life.

As you connect with this possibility, notice what happens to your hands and feet. You're free to move now. You're able to use your hands, feet, and mind for something other than fighting anxiety.

To Feel Is to Be Human

People struggling with anxiety problems are some of the strongest people we know. They're survivors. But they can also be very harsh with themselves. They feel that they're not good enough, they're too weak, they're not trying hard enough, they just haven't got what it takes to lead a more fulfilled life.

What does your mind tell you about you and your anxiety problem? How does your mind beat you up? Jot down a few thoughts that come to mind.

_____

_____

_____

_____

_____

_____

_____

Here's the thing: You don't have to argue with your mind. It's a choice you make. Don't get stuck here trying to convince yourself of anything. Just know that it's your mind doing what minds do: trying to make things better, or to protect you, the best way it knows how. When such thoughts show up, thank your mind for each of them. Then move on.

Let's try that out now. How would you have thanked your mind for these thoughts? Be creative.

_____

_____

_____

_____

_____

_____

One of the most profound things about being a human is that we get to experience all our emotions. From the happiest to the most sorrowful, each is a valuable aspect of being alive.

You can practice this skill the next time you find anxiety getting loud. Just say, "Thank you, Mind," when anxiety thoughts come up, to allow them to just be there without taking over everything. And then move on. Give it a try.

Close your eyes and gently guide your attention to the natural rhythm of your breath in your chest and belly. After a few moments, write about something painful or hurtful, perhaps a recent event or a time in which you felt very anxious.

_____

_____

_____

_____

_____

_____

_____

_____

_____

_____

_____

Now read what you wrote. Take in that negativity and painful upset. Breathe in the discomfort.

Now imagine people. People who are feeling what you're feeling in this very moment. After all, you're not alone in this. It's likely being felt by millions of people all over this world.

Using your visualization skills, try to pick out one or a few people, from any point in time. See in your mind's eye that they are feeling exactly what you're feeling. What do you notice about them? How can you tell that they feel as you do?

Keep imagining your fellow anxiety sufferers. And now, breathe—and on each inhale, breathe in their discomfort. Do this for them. On each exhale, breathe out relief, joyfulness, and goodwill for them, along with the wish that they, like you, be free of suffering with anxiety.

Do it slowly, with the natural rhythm of your breathing. Continue to connect with your pain as you breathe in, and with each out-breath, expend goodwill and a wish that others may find relief from the suffering they get caught in when they experience hurt and discomfort.

If you could share some of your wisdom and comfort with them, what would you say? How could you help them so they no longer have to push the worries, anxieties, and fears away?

_____

_____

_____

_____

_____

_____

_____

_____

_____

Now look over what you wrote. Are you willing to say some of these kind words to yourself the next time your anxiety spikes? This is something you can do anytime, anywhere.

Feeling the Limits of Control

Life has taught you how well control works. As a child, you probably avoided touching a hot stove because it hurt to touch it. You may have learned this the hard way or by listening to your parents or caregivers warning you about the consequences: "Don't touch, because you'll get hurt." Keeping your hand away from hot things kept you safe and prevented injury.

Take a moment to think about a situation or two where this has been true in your experience. Write about them.

How has this same idea worked for your anxiety?

_____

_____

_____

_____

_____

_____

_____

_____

_____

_____

What you've learned again and again is that control works to help you avoid and reduce external sources of pain and harm. Naturally then, these strategies ought to work when you apply them to internal sources of pain and hurt. Unfortunately, that's not how it works.

You cannot control your anxiety by running away from, avoiding, or suppressing unwanted sensations, feelings, thoughts, worries, or images—as much as you may want to.

What Really Matters?

What matters to you? Most people don't think about it until it's too late to do something about it. We don't want to see that happen to you. It's important in your anxiety journey to connect with what you want to be about in this life.

> You won't be able to see the costs of the anxiety struggle in your life unless you can see what you want to be about and do in this life.

We know that this may seem drastic, but we'd like you to imagine that you're observing your own funeral. Visualize yourself in an open casket. Visualize the flowers and music. What can you describe? Be as specific as possible.

_____

_____

_____

_____

_____

_____

Look around the room. Who do you see?

_____

_____

_____

_____

_____

_____

What conversations can you hear? What are your partner, your kids, your best friend, your colleagues, and your neighbors saying about you? Listen carefully to each of them as they say what they have to say.

Really immerse yourself. Sit back, close your eyes, imagine the honest impressions of your funeral day and what others have to say... Then write.

What I heard people say about me was...

_____

_____

_____

_____

_____

_____

And now, in your heart of hearts, what did you *want* to hear people say about your life?

What I wanted to hear people say about me was...

_____

_____

_____

_____

_____

_____

_____

There's something critically important in what you heard and wrote down a moment ago. What you heard others say about you was based on what they see you doing or not doing. But what you *wanted* to hear them say about you is based on what you really want your life to be about.

Anxiety is costly precisely because it gets in the way of what you want to do. It turns the things you wish to hear said about you into the things that actually get said about you, like "She never went out" or "He never traveled to see his family."

The good news is that your life isn't over yet. You still have time to *do* things to be the type of person you want to be. You can start living the way you want to be remembered later on.

Write your epitaph (the inscription on your gravestone) as it would be written if you were to die today. What would it say if it was about what you've been doing in the service of managing your anxiety? What have you become by living in the service of your anxieties?

Here lies _____,

who _____

_____

_____

_____

_____

_____

Now let's flip it. Imagine that you could live your life free of any worry, anxiety, or fear. Wouldn't that be something? What would you do? What is it you want to be remembered for?

_____

_____

_____

_____

_____

Now think of a phrase or series of brief statements that would capture the essence of the life you want to lead for a new headstone.

Here lies _____ ,

who _____

_____

_____

_____

_____

_____

_____

Which epitaph do you want to be known for? Which one is more vital to you? Which best fits your life now?

Right now, you can estimate how much time you have left on this planet. First, calculate how many days you've already lived by multiplying your current age in years by 365.

Age now in days: _____

After you get that number, subtract it from 29,200. (That's how many days you'd have lived by eighty years old.) This new number is an estimate of the number of days you likely have left to live.

Days left: _____

Again, this isn't to scare you. It's to wake you up to your life as is—as it's passing in every moment. And it's to get you thinking about how you've been spending this precious time—and how you *want* to spend it.

Right now, thinking about the ideal epitaph you wrote for yourself, consider:

How do I want to use the time I have left?

_____

_____

_____

_____

_____

_____

How do I want to use the next year?

_____

_____

_____

_____

_____

_____

How do I want to use the next month?

_____

_____

_____

_____

_____

How do I want to use the next week?

_____

_____

_____

_____

_____

How do I want to use tomorrow?

_____

_____

_____

_____

How you use your time and energy is a choice that you can make and something you can control.

You've Done This Before

If you look closely, you'll see that as you take steps in the direction you want to go, you'll probably get something that you don't want to have—unpleasant feelings and bodily sensations.

To move into your life, you need to let go of the urge to act on your discomfort while moving into and with your internal experiences, just as they are. This can be difficult to do, just like many other things in life that are potentially good for you.

Recall some vital and important things that you do now and that were once difficult to do. Think simple and expand out. For example, what was it like when you first learned how to eat with a fork and knife, or use a toilet? How about when you first started learning your ABCs, writing letters of the alphabet and eventually your name? How about learning how to read or use money? Pick one experience and describe it.

_____

_____

_____

_____

_____

How difficult was it initially? How did you struggle?

_____

_____

_____

_____

_____

_____

_____

And how did you ultimately overcome your difficulty? What did that moment feel like?

_____

_____

_____

_____

_____

_____

_____

Could you draw upon those capacities and those reserves of strength and ability again? Chances are, yes!

Your life up until now has been a journey of small moments. The things that you do and want out of life often start out seeming difficult or impossible. And to do the things you want to do calls on you to move with and through difficult moments, often many times. But with willingness, and the ability to notice what you feel *and to let go of trying to control it*, you can do this.

> To have it all, you must be willing to have it all—the good, the unpleasant, and the sometimes ugly moments that life offers and similar experiences that arise from within you.

Comfort in Your Own Skin

Most of us don't like what we see when we look at ourselves in the mirror. There's always something about our bodies that could be different or better. The same is true of our sense of who we are—the part of us that is more than the parts of our physical body. It can be uncomfortable to see yourself exposed.

Learning to be with yourself, just as you are, involves embracing your vulnerabilities and imperfections. Learning to accept yourself, just as you are, and to allow whatever is in your experience to just be there, is also key to cultivating peace of mind—and developing the skill of approaching what you fear instead of avoiding it. This skill is particularly important in your interactions with other people.

Try looking at yourself in front of a full-length mirror for two to five minutes. This will be more powerful if you can do it undressed and fully exposed. It will probably bring up some things for you that are uncomfortable.

Take a moment to look at yourself, really look. What do you see? What's it like to stand with yourself, unmasked, just as you are? Write down any sensations coming from your body or any thoughts that cross your mind.

_____

_____

_____

_____

_____

_____

_____

_____

_____

Shift your attention to your head and face. Notice the top of your head—your hair and skin. What does it really look like? Study it, noticing the textures, shape, and colors. Then gradually move to your face—eyes, nose, mouth, and cheeks.

What do you want to *do* with your seeing eyes, hearing ears, or your lips and mouth over the course of your life? See if you can allow yourself to be with your experience and let your mind do its own thing. Then write about your experience.

_____

_____

_____

_____

_____

Turning back to your body, notice that each part of your body is a part of you. Each has its own story to tell. What is your mind telling you about them now? Perhaps you'll find regret, shame, embarrassment, humiliation, or thoughts such as "too big," "too small," "ugly," "beautiful," "wrinkled," "smooth," "attractive," or "unattractive." What are you experiencing?

Allow yourself time to just notice the labels your mind may be giving you. Then see if you can focus back on the raw, unedited experience of you. Notice any inner discomfort that may show up. See if you can be with your discomfort as you spend this time with you. Allow yourself to be with you just as you are: whole...complete...unique...perfectly imperfect...and vulnerable... like everyone else.

See yourself from a kind perspective—there's nothing to be fixed, no need to hide anything. You are you. Allow all that is to simply be what it is, as you do the things you wish to do.

Working with Sensations

Now let's look at one of the uncomfortable sensations that comes up when you're feeling anxious. Think about one bodily sensation that's particularly difficult or intense for you. Describe it and the times when it typically comes up.

_____

_____

_____

_____

_____

_____

Now take a moment to just acknowledge the sensation. Say to yourself,

There is _____. *Or, There's my* _____.
[insert the uncomfortable sensation]

This is the perfect time to lean into the discomfort and invite it in, as best you can.

I will allow my _____ *to be what it is, a feeling in my body, nothing more and nothing less.*

Where else have you experienced this one sensation? Notice that you've had this sensation before when you haven't been anxious or afraid. Write about what that felt like.

_____

_____

_____

_____

_____

_____

_____

Now, the next time this sensation comes up when you're anxious, how can you make space for it?

_____

_____

_____

_____

_____

_____

_____

_____

What does this sensation *really* feel like? Where does it start and where does it end?

_____

_____

_____

_____

_____

_____

Is this particular feeling or physical sensation really your enemy, or can you just have it as a feeling, a sensation? **YES   NO**

Is this sensation something you must not or cannot have? Even if your mind tells you that you can't have it, how willing are you to open up a space for it in your heart?

_____

_____

_____

_____

_____

_____

Is this something you absolutely must struggle with, or is there room inside you to feel all that and stay with it? How can you make your inside space a kind space?

_____

_____

_____

_____

_____

_____

As you make space for each sensation, one by one, you may notice that your mind is feeding you all sorts of labels—old F.E.A.R. (False Evidence Appearing Real) labels—like "dangerous," "getting worse," or "out of control." When that happens, simply thank your mind for such labels and then gently shift your attention back to watching and noticing with gentle curiosity, openness, and compassion.

Thank you, mind, for _____

_____

_____

_____

_____

Facing your discomfort with kind and gentle willingness is where you have your power. And it's a necessary and helpful step out of anxiety and into a more vital life.

PART 3

Doing

Finding Your North Star

As Joseph Campbell teaches us, happiness flows from listening to your heart and then doing things that matter.

To create the conditions for genuine happiness in your life, you'll first need to know what matters to you—what your bliss or passion is. Next, you'll need to find ways to do what matters in your daily life—using the skills of *noticing* what comes up and simply *allowing* it to be there—without letting anxiety stop you.

Imagine you could spend your time doing anything.

If _____ **wasn't such a problem for me,**

  [your biggest anxiety- or fear-related concern]

I'd be doing _____

_____.

- What does whatever it is you wrote down *represent* for you? Is it freedom? A great connection with others? Creativity? Growth? Purpose? Learning? Achievement? Listen to your heart for the answer.

- Now come up with a single word that captures the essence of what you wrote down: _____. This is your North Star.

- Or, well, one of your North Stars. Try this a couple more times, if you like—each time with a different anxiety symptom and a different dream.

If _____ **wasn't such a problem for me,**

[your biggest anxiety- or fear-related concern]

I'd be doing _____

_____ .

- What does whatever it is you wrote down *represent* for you? Is it freedom? A great connection with others? Creativity? Growth? Purpose? Learning? Achievement? Listen to your heart for the answer.

- Now come up with a single word that captures the essence of what you wrote down: _____. This is your North Star.

If _____ **wasn't such a problem for me,**

[your biggest anxiety- or fear-related concern]

I'd be doing _____

_____ .

- What does whatever it is you wrote down *represent* for you? Is it freedom? A great connection with others? Creativity? Growth? Purpose? Learning? Achievement? Listen to your heart for the answer.

- Now come up with a single word that captures the essence of what you wrote down: _____. This is your North Star.

These North Stars are statements of your values. You can refer to them the next time anxiety happens. When you find yourself in a tough spot, itching to avoid something you think will make you anxious, see if you can remind yourself of your values and let go of control, so you can do something new.

Try plotting out these three North Stars. You can call them your "Values Constellation." And, like the North Star existing within the Little Dipper, this constellation can always point you in the direction that means the most to you.

Looking Around
Your North Star

Your values, your North Stars, ultimately guide how you live your life with anxiety. But they do shift and change within all the different aspects of life. Let's look more closely at important areas of your life and take a moment to reflect on how you would like to express your North Stars within them.

Keep in mind that some areas may be more important to you than others. Also, for some of these areas, there may be something you can do to express your North Star right away; for others, you may simply need time.

Career

How would you like to use your energy, talents, and skills productively? What would that look like? What would you do if you could be doing anything? Describe the qualities of a job or endeavor that you believe would be perfect for you.

_____

_____

_____

_____

_____

What do you want your work or career to be about or stand for? What is important to you about your work (for example, financial security, intellectual challenge, independence, prestige, interacting with or helping people)?

_____

_____

_____

_____

Relationships

What type of romantic relationship would you like to have? How do you want to treat your partner or a person with whom you share a special commitment and bond? How would you want to be treated by them?

_____

_____

_____

_____

Take a moment now to consider your relationships with members of the family in which you were raised. Are your family bonds important to you? Do they give you a sense of meaning and purpose? Are these roles and relationships important to you, and if so, how?

How do you want to interact with your family members now? If you have siblings or stepsiblings, what type of stepsister or stepbrother do you want to be? If your parent(s) is/are alive, what type of son or daughter do you want to be?

If you have kids, what type of parent do you want to be?

How do you want to act to support your role as a parent?

_____

_____

_____

_____

What personal qualities would you like to develop in and through your relationships?

_____

_____

_____

_____

_____

_____

How would you interact with your friends if you were the "ideal you" with them?

_____

_____

_____

_____

_____

Personal Growth

Look within yourself and see if you can find anything about personal growth and learning that's important to you. Would you like to sharpen skills you already have, or develop new ones? Are there areas of competence you'd like to explore?

_____

_____

_____

_____

_____

Health

How and why do you take care of yourself? How do you want to take care of your body and your health (for example, through what you eat, by exercising, or by being physically fit)? How important is physical health to you?

_____

_____

_____

_____

_____

Think about what motivates you to stay healthy. What is it about caring for your mental well-being that's appealing to you, and how important is it to you to act in accordance with this value?

_____

_____

_____

_____

_____

_____

_____

Spirituality

What seems most appropriate and suitable for you? Are there things larger than your own life that inspire you? What are the mysteries of life before which you stand in awe? In what (if anything) do you have faith?

_____

_____

_____

_____

_____

Describe the role you'd like to see spirituality play in your life and how that would manifest. If you had this in your life, what kind of qualities would it provide for you?

_____

_____

_____

_____

_____

_____

Community and Legacy

How would you like to share your talents and passions in your community? What pulls at your heart here?

_____

_____

_____

_____

_____

_____

Is anything currently missing in this area of your life? What can you do to make the world a better place? Why are community activities (such as volunteering, voting, recycling) important to you?

_____

_____

_____

_____

Play

Look for the value you place on expressing that playful spirit. Do you cherish having time to unwind, have fun, be a kid again, challenge yourself, or develop new interests or skills, like playing a musical instrument? Any activity that has a playful quality to it counts here. So how would you describe the quality of this part of your life if it were exactly the way you would like it to be?

_____

_____

_____

_____

_____

And with that in mind, what activities, interests, or hobbies would you love to cultivate and explore if you could? How do you nurture yourself through hobbies, sports, or play?

Anything Else?

As you reflected on areas of your life, did other important values show up? If they did, write them in the space below.

Are You Living Your Values Now?

As you've discovered from the previous activity, you can break down life into a few different important areas: career, relationships, play, health, personal growth, community, and spirituality. Take a moment to pick one of these areas that's especially important to you—and where your anxiety typically makes itself known. Select one that you find particularly important to you in this moment.

Write your value here: _____

_____

_____

What are your intentions?

_____

_____

_____

_____

_____

_____

_____

Are you currently doing what matters to you?

If yes, then how does that feel?

_____

_____

_____

_____

_____

If no, why not?

_____

_____

_____

_____

_____

What stands in your way? Here, it can be helpful to break the anxiety barriers down. Let's look separately at the thoughts and images, sensations, feelings, and urges and impulses that are getting in your way.

Thoughts and images: What thoughts or images show up that get in the way of you living out your valued intentions?

_____

_____

_____

_____

_____

_____

_____

Feelings: What emotions get in the way of you taking action for your valued intentions?

_____

_____

_____

_____

_____

_____

_____

Physical sensations: What are the physical sensations in your body that seem to stand between you and what matters to you?

_____

_____

_____

_____

_____

_____

Urges and impulses: What urges or impulses get in your way? Are you shutting down? Turning away? Do you use and abuse alcohol or other substances?

_____

_____

_____

_____

_____

_____

You live out your values in the actions you take, and these will make your life worthwhile. "Managing my anxiety" isn't a value; it's no way to live. Instead, when anxiety arises, you can notice, allow, and do. You can reconnect with your heart and follow your bliss, even when life is unkind!

You're the Creator of Your Life

You already know what it's like when you turn your life over to fear and anxiety. You don't get to live it. But here's the deal. You are the master and creator of your life.

Your values will motivate you to go forward and take steps in a more vital, meaningful direction—one where you, and not your anxiety, are in charge. It is from this place that you create a life that's truly in alignment with your core. You gain the power to choose how you respond to the fear, the dark images from your past, or the sense of foreboding about an uncertain future. It is you who can decide to fight the war with anxiety or to make peace with it.

The next time you go through an anxious moment—and find anxiety taking control—come back to this journal. Describe what happened.

What did you choose to do? Or did you just react with old habits? (No judgment here, but do be honest.)

If you had a do-over—a mindful one this time—what would you choose to do and attend to?

Anxiety happens. Remember that it's not a choice whether it comes or not. But it's your choice what you do with it. You can choose to fight it or you can choose to get curious about it, open up to it, and let it be. Like waves on the ocean, anxiety will pass.

And, in the moments you might "fail"—that is, fall short of what you might *want* to do—remember that "failure" is a judgment about outcomes that are unknown because they are in the future, not now. And when it comes to outcomes, remember that values aren't things you do or don't achieve. They're qualities you can express in your actions that will help motivate you and serve as a decision-making guide. When you fall and fail to keep your commitments, you can acknowledge what happened, recommit to your values, and come back to following your North Stars.

In the moment I did not act on my values, I felt _____

_____

_____

_____

_____

_____

_____

_____ *and that's okay.*

In these moments, I can be kind and gentle with myself by _____

And of course, another thing you can do is to *do the opposite* of whatever it is anxiety might tell you to do. If you were to have done the opposite in the situation you were in, what would that have looked like?

This next exercise can be really good for finding your way back to your values, even when anxiety's pull is strongest. It works best if you are in the middle of a specific anxious experience.

Go ahead and take a few moments to get in touch with your breath and the gentle rising and falling of your breath in your chest and belly.

Rest in the truth of your experience with each natural breath, and become aware of what shows up that has been hard for you. It could be a troubling thought, worry, image, or intense bodily sensation. Describe how this makes you feel.

_____

_____

_____

_____

_____

_____

Gently, directly, and firmly shift your attention on and into the discomfort, no matter how bad it seems. Stay with your discomfort, breathe with it, and see if you can gently open up to it and make space for it. With each new breath, imagine that you are creating more and more space for this anxiety barrier to simply be there.

Is this feeling or thought really your enemy? Or can you have it, notice it, own it, and let it be? Can you make room for the discomfort, for the tension, for the anxiety? What does it really feel like to allow it to be there, moment to moment? Is this something you *must* struggle with, or can you invite the discomfort in, saying to yourself, *I welcome you in because you are just a part of my experience right now?*

_____

_____

_____

_____

_____

_____

Stay with your discomfort for as long as it pulls on your attention.

As you sink more deeply into this moment of just being where you are, see if you can be present with your values and commitments.

Why am I here?

_____

_____

_____

_____

_____

Where do I want to go?

_____

_____

_____

_____

_____

What do I want to be about in my life in this moment?

_____

_____

_____

_____

_____

_____

Remember that mindful allowing is a skill that will give you freedom to live your values. Like a seedling, it needs to be watered regularly to grow.

Bringing Compassion to Your Anxiety

Compassion and kindness can literally take the sting out of anxiety, panic, fear, and worry. This will transform your roadblocks into something you can live with and move with on your way toward your values.

To develop compassion, you must cultivate your capacity for loving-kindness, just like that of a mother toward her newborn child. Like a muscle, it is a skill that will grow with practice.

Treating yourself kindly is particularly important when you feel tired, stressed, or lonely, and are craving things like nurturing, praise, stimulation, food, or drugs. These TLC problems can be undercut if you remind yourself to meet them with compassion and kindness wrapped in tender loving care.

Maybe you'd like to be kinder to yourself, but you don't know how to start. Here's something to do: make a commitment to practice at least one act of kindness toward yourself every day. For the next three days, try starting each day with this commitment.

... *Day 1* ...

My anxiety
level is:

10
9
8
7
6
5
4
3
2
1
0

What is something I could do to be kind to myself?

If I'm feeling anxious, how would this moment of kindness help?

I pledge to follow through on this self-kindness.

I will be kind to myself at _____ am/pm.

(If you can, set an exact time to be kind to yourself.)

Date: _____

My anxiety
level is:

10
9
8
7
6
5
4
3
2
1
0

What is something I could do to be kind to myself?

If I'm feeling anxious, how would this moment of
kindness help?

I pledge to follow through on this self-kindness.

I will be kind to myself at _____ am/pm.

(If you can, set an exact time to be kind to yourself.)

147

Date: _____

My anxiety
level is:

10
9
8
7
6
5
4
3
2
1
0

What is something I could do to be kind to myself?

If I'm feeling anxious, how would this moment of kindness help?

I pledge to follow through on this self-kindness.

I will be kind to myself at _____ am/pm.

(If you can, set an exact time to be kind to yourself.)

Compassion and kindness are not feelings. They're actions.

Coming Up with a
Kindness Mantra

Here's a tip: if you're ever feeling really stressed, close your eyes, touch your forehead or your chest, and think of the hand of a caregiver touching you when you were young and sick. You can bring to mind anyone else who left you feeling good, loved, and cared for. The kindness of this caring person's hand is alive in yours. And you can give that kindness to yourself, right now and anytime, anywhere.

It's time to develop a personal kindness mantra. It ought to be simple and important to you. If you feel a pang of resistance to a phrase, try a different one until you find one that resonates with you. For instance, you may come up with a phrase such as:

May I have peace.

May I be kind.

May I experience joy.

May I be free of suffering.

Take a moment to come up with your own personal phrase:

May I _____

You can also have a few in a row.

May I _____

May I _____

May I _____

As you walk and move about your day, silently repeat your personal loving-kindness phrases. And then, when you find your attention being pulled by something or someone outside of you, gently bring your awareness to whatever it was that caught your attention, and then silently extend your personal phrase to that object, person, or creature. Then come back to yourself, and so on.

Coming Up with Valued Goals

Again, the journey of your life is made up of the steps you take—what you do. Each and every step will move you either closer to or farther away from what matters to you. And values, as you learned, act like a beacon as you take your steps. They point you toward what's important. This is crucial when you feel pulled and pushed around in a sea of worry, anxiety, panic, and doom and gloom.

A necessary complement to values are goals. Where values are the broad directions you want your life to go in, *goals* are the concrete, achievable tasks you embark on to ensure you live out those values. Think of goals as steps on a valued path.

Take a second to think of one of your values—one you want to manifest more wholeheartedly in your life. Write it down, in broad strokes.

_____

_____

Now consider one goal you'd like to achieve that reflects this value. How can you make this goal **specific** (concrete, practical)?

_____

_____

_____

How can you make this goal **meaningful** (reflecting what truly matters to you)?

_____

_____

_____

_____

_____

_____

How can you make this goal **active** (something that you can do and have control over)?

_____

_____

_____

_____

_____

_____

How can you make this goal **realistic?** That is, does it work with your current life situation?

_____

_____

_____

How can you make this goal **time-framed** (something you can put in your calendar)?

And, above all, does this goal truly lead you in the direction of your **valued intentions**? Does it express what matters to you, what you want to be about and become?

Having settled on a goal, you've put the first guideposts on your road map. Now focus on the incremental steps you need to take to get there. Start with a short-term goal and break it down into smaller intermediate steps. Think of each step you need to take to attain your goal. Then write down those steps.

Now think about a logical order for the steps. What needs to happen first before the other steps can follow? If no particular order is necessary, then start with the easiest step.

1. _____

2. _____

3. _____

4. _____

5. _____

6. _____

7. _____

8. _____

9. _____

10. _____

Now it's time to make a commitment. Start with step 1.

I will _____ *at* _____ *on* _____.

       [insert step]   [time]   [day]

Think of someone you can tell about achieving your goal once you've done so.

I will call or text _____.

Dealing with Barriers

All along you've been working to get clear about anxiety barriers that get in the way of living your life. Most of the barriers we've covered arise from within you. But there's another set of obstacles that can trip you up. We call them *external barriers*, such as lack of money, time, skills, or the necessary information to do what matters. The good news is that it doesn't really matter if the barriers are inside or outside of you. What's most important is that you develop a plan.

Bring to mind one of your valued intentions—the things you care about in your heart and want to be about.

_____

_____

_____

_____

_____

Imagine for a moment that nothing gets in your way and that you're free to do what you really, truly care about. See yourself being about something that matters in your heart. See yourself living out those intentions as if watching yourself on a giant movie screen. What are you doing? Describe the scenes in detail.

Focus on the very first step or two, just as you decide to act. Notice where you are. Notice what you're saying. Notice what you're doing with your hands and feet. And, if other people are involved, watch how they might be responding to you.

And now, take an inventory of what's showing up inside of you. Observe what your mind is telling you. Is there judgment about you, or the situation, or other people? Do you notice blocking thoughts, like, *I can't do this...it's too much?* Or discouraging thoughts, like, *Nothing matters...so don't bother.* Or maybe your mind is conjuring up images of catastrophe, old wounds, doom and gloom. Or maybe it's telling you something else, like, *I don't have enough time.* Just notice what's there and take stock.

Now move on to what's going on in your body. What are you feeling?

Now look and see if your mind is commanding you to do something. Is it telling you to cut and run, turn away, lash out, or give up? Just notice these urges and impulses, and write them out.

_____

_____

_____

_____

_____

_____

Now see yourself acting on that value just as you wish *and* with nothing standing in your way. You're free of barriers and successful in doing what you set out to do. What is the feeling like? What does success feel like on the inside? Notice any thoughts, emotions, and physical sensations. Describe the internal experience.

_____

_____

_____

_____

_____

_____

Stay with this image, and when you're ready, shift your attention to the world around you—the people, the events, and the environment that surround you in this scenario. What's different? How does it feel to be freed up from an old barrier? How does it feel to freely do something you've been afraid to do?

_____

_____

_____

_____

_____

_____

When you're ready to wrap up, open your eyes and jot down all of the positive outcomes you discovered during this exercise. Let them serve as a reminder to you of what is possible as you embark on your journey.

_____

_____

_____

_____

_____

_____

> You cultivate genuine happiness by being more willing, open, and allowing with your mind, body, and everything your history throws at you. You also create joy by practicing being gentle, kind, and mindful as you do what you want to do.

Once in a while, you may take longer to reach a goal than you had hoped. All of this and more is just fine. We all move at our own pace. The most important thing is that you keep yourself moving forward in vital ways. You can draw upon the strategies and skills you've learned in previous chapters when discomfort *difficulty* threatens to get in the way of discomfort *vitality*.

Making Peace with a Difficult Past

Your anxiety has likely caused you hurt and pain. And there are probably things you've done because of your anxiety for which you might wish to be forgiven or to forgive.

When people hear the word "forgiveness," they often jump to conclusions. You may too. Your mind may tell you that forgiveness means condoning or forgetting past wrongs, or worse, ignoring the hurt and pain you may have suffered at the hands of someone else, or even pain that was self-inflicted. You may see forgiveness as a sign of weakness or as something that you must feel inside before you take steps to forgive. None of these are true. It's nothing more than letting go of a painful past so that you can heal and move on.

First, take a few moments to acknowledge hurt and pain as it is, without judgment or denial. What cost has your anxiety born on your life?

_____

_____

_____

_____

_____

Take a step back. How would your perspective of your anxiety change if you decided to acknowledge that the pain it caused was not anxiety's fault, but just anxiety's nature? Anxiety does what it does. The good news is that it is always your choice how you respond to that perspective. One helpful and life-affirming choice is to offer compassion and kindness to your situation. How could you specifically extend some compassion to the pain your anxiety has caused? Be creative.

Kindness and compassion are shown by your actions —how you relate to your mind, body, and life. Kindness and compassion will help you heal and move with your anxiety instead of remaining stuck, struggling with old wounds.

Now write a forgiveness letter to your anxiety. Release all of your grudges and resentments.

Dear Anxiety,

You can let go of holding on to the wish and hope for a resolution. You can take the energy and effort focused on resolving, fighting back, or getting even and put it to more vital use. You can bring kindness to your experience by facing your pain squarely for what it is. Own it because it is yours, and then choose to let it go.

Becoming Aware of Hurts Beneath Painful Memories

You have a past. Everyone does. It is full of moments: dark, bright, and neutral. Some of it is sweet, and other parts are bitter, even extremely so. What you remember can leave you feeling more alive or torn apart and wounded. There are many ways to get stuck in the past.

It's very hard to go forward in life when you're always looking back. The key is to keep your eyes and heart looking forward from right where you are, in the present.

For this next exercise, you will need a candle, a way to light it, and a place to sit. Go ahead and light the candle and then get in a comfortable position in your chair. As you watch the flicker of the candle flame, bring your attention to the gentle rising and falling of your breath in your chest and belly. Take a few minutes to center yourself as you breathe in and out.

Now allow your awareness to shift to a painful memory or anxious experience. See if you can allow yourself to visualize the scene fully, as if you are watching a movie in slow motion. What happened? Describe in detail.

_____

_____

_____

_____

Now turn to your candle. Watch the flame as you acknowledge the painful situation unfolding in your mind's eye. As best as you can, open up to all of it: the hurt, pain, sadness, regret, loss, and resentment. Allow yourself to become aware of your hurt and painful emotions, and simply acknowledge the hurt you experienced and the hurt you may have caused. There's no need to resist or fight or blame. Simply acknowledge and become aware of your past experience.

Now visualize the person or event that inflicted the hurt. As you begin to do so, allow the person or event to drift over and become the candle. If it was you who caused harm, then see yourself as the candle. Focus on the candle and continue to visualize the person or situation that hurt you or caused the hurt. If it helps, you can visualize the action that hurt you as the flame, and the person or situation who committed the hurt as the candle. If you were the source of hurt, then let your actions become the flame and you the candle.

Notice that the flame is not the candle. The actions of the person who hurt you are not the same as the person who committed them. As you breathe in and out, give yourself time to connect with this difference. Then, bring each hurtful action into the flame one by one and notice it, label it, and then see the difference between the hurtful action and the person. Visualize what was done, not who did it.

Finally, bring your attention back to the human being in the candle—the perpetrator of wrongs against you, or those you may have committed yourself. Try writing about how that person is also a human being and vulnerable to harm just like you are. At a basic human level, the two of you are not that different. Connect with that person's hardships, losses, missed opportunities, poor choices, faults and failings, hurts and sadness, and hopes and dreams—without condoning their actions. See if you can connect with that person's humanity and imperfections as you connect with your own humanity and imperfections, hardships, loss, pain, and suffering.

Now you're ready to try to extend forgiveness, let go, and move on. See if you can bring into awareness what your life would be like if you let go of all the negative energy you are holding on to—your grievances, grudges, bitterness, and anger. What would it be like to let go of the effort needed to shut out this painful experience from your past?

_____

_____

_____

_____

When you're ready, bring into your awareness how you have needed other people's forgiveness in the past. Imagine extending that forgiveness to the person who hurt or offended you. What could you say to that person?

_____

_____

_____

_____

_____

Gently extend your hands as you say,

> "In forgiving you, I forgive myself. In letting go of my pain and anger toward you, I bring peace and freedom to myself. I invite peace and compassion into my life and into my hurt and pain. I choose to let go of this burden that I have been carrying for so long."

Repeat these phrases slowly as you extend forgiveness.

The Movie of Your Life

As you continue working to notice and stay open to your experience, even when anxiety is there, you'll probably run into a lot of old stories about yourself and who you "are." Let's take some time to think about the life movie that your mind feeds you most often. Imagine that you're watching your past on a big movie screen. What experiences and events make up your story? What events or experiences does your mind gravitate toward and use to tell the story of you now?

Your Life Movie, Take 1

Go ahead and write the story about you that your mind naturally comes up with. It's okay if the things you come up with include mostly dark moments from your past. It's okay if that's not the case. Just write it all down as if no one will know. Let it pour out. No editing.

_____

_____

_____

_____

_____

_____

_____

_____

_____

_____

_____

_____

_____

Now pause and take a few slow breaths, and then read, slowly and out loud, what you wrote down.

As you do, be mindful that you can observe the script. Be the "observer you" and just notice. What kind of story is being told?

How does this story grab and hook you? Is there anything in there that you absolutely cannot think about *now*? Is there anything you're experiencing now that's really your enemy?

Just notice, and see if you can open up and be a kind and impartial observer.

Your Life Movie, Take 2

Now we'd like you to write another script. Keep in the facts from Take 1, the events that actually happened. But this time, we want you to add to the story. What experiences were missing the first time around? What else could be added?

Does this revised story feel different? Does it grab and hook you in the same way as the first? Is there anything about the script that you cannot have or experience *now*?

Your Life Movie, Take 3

Now, if you're willing, we'd like to invite you to repeat this exercise at least one more time. Again, keep what you have in Take 2, and add to that with experiences you've had—including ones that might be far removed in time, and may not have come to mind the first time you did this—as well as insights you've gained from the revisions you just made. Give yourself about five minutes to write, and then continue the exercise.

Look over what you have just written. Notice the words, letters, and ink on the page. Simply observe what's there with a sense of kindness, curiosity, and gentleness. And consider: is there anything about the story that you cannot have or experience *now*?

Moving Toward a Valued Life— Even When Anxiety Happens

There'll be times when you find the voice of your anxiety is getting loud and keeping you from doing what you want to be doing. When that happens, refer to this list of strategies.

1. **Freshen up your mindfulness and meditation practices.** You can switch between the two exercises. You can also practice in places other than your usual spot. Also look for new exercises in books, online, and on various apps. Or you can create new exercises yourself.

2. **When you're stuck in a rut, step out of that rut and do something different and new.** Imagine life is like a menu giving you many different offerings. Don't order the same thing every time. Consider all the options and choose something different. Step out of your ruts and follow your bliss.

3. **Continue reading and learning.** Expand your knowledge about mindfulness, meditation, and the approach to anxiety you've learned about in this book—which comes from acceptance and commitment therapy, a form of therapy in which you practice psychological flexibility in the face of anxiety, stress, and other such internal experiences in order to move yourself toward your North Stars—the things you truly value.

4. Feed your mind and life with uplifting experiences. Give yourself a break from the news, the Internet, social media, and other sources of stimulation. Turn off screens and choose quiet time away from the negative noise of the world around you. Stillness creates opportunities for peace and gives you space to think and move. Or do something enriching, such as doing something aligned with your values, reading uplifting stories, spending time in nature, listening to music, or making or looking at art.

5. Nurture a spirit of playfulness with your mind, body, and life. Study after study shows that adults who practice being more playful with themselves and others—and make time for fun and play—are generally happier and healthier, and live longer too. Think about the things you like to do that are playful and fun, and see if you can build a spirit of play into your life—physically, mentally, and emotionally. You may be pleasantly surprised at what it offers you.

There's also a process of self-exploration you can use whenever you encounter barriers and you're unsure whether your planned action is good for you. Ask yourself some questions:

If this thought (or emotion, bodily state, or memory) I'm experiencing could give advice, would the advice point me forward in my life or keep me stuck?

If I think of a core value of mine, what guidance would that value give me right now?

What would I advise my child or someone I love to do in this situation?

If others could see what I am doing now, would they see me doing things that I value?

In what valued direction have my feet taken me when I listened to this advice?

What does my experience tell me about this solution? And what do I trust more: my mind and feelings, or my experience?

_____

_____

_____

_____

_____

_____

How can I best keep on moving with my barriers toward a valued life?

_____

_____

_____

_____

_____

_____

_____

Is what I am doing now moving me forward or backward in my life?

> **A meaningful life is built one step at a time.**

Is what I am doing now what I want to be about? And what do I want to be about?

Asking questions like these when you're faced with adversity and doubt is far more helpful than listening to what your unwise anxious mind comes up with or what the surging impulses seem to be telling you.

The Last Word

Finally, before we end, what do you have to say to your anxiety?

Write a letter to it. Let it know how you feel once and for all.

Notice, Allow, and Do

As you move forward in your life, remember that you have everything you need, even when your mind tells you otherwise. Your emotional life is a gift, and strong feelings like anxiety and fear may be there to alert you to what you care about. After all, when you feel strongly, it often means that you care strongly. Your anxiety may also signal to you when you are moving away from the life you wish to live. Remember that you can feel what you feel and still do what you care about. Your willingness to do that, in small and large ways, is what will add up to your life.

We wish you the very best on your journey!

John P. Forsyth, PhD, is professor of psychology, and director of the anxiety disorders research program at the University at Albany, SUNY. Forsyth is a highly sought-after speaker, acceptance and commitment therapy (ACT) workshop leader, and member of the teaching faculty at the Omega Institute for Holistic Studies, the Esalen Institute, and 1440 Multiversity. His teachings and writing focus on how to use ACT and mindfulness practices to alleviate suffering, awaken the human spirit, and cultivate well-being. He is coauthor of *The Mindfulness and Acceptance Workbook for Anxiety* and *Anxiety Happens*.

Georg H. Eifert, PhD, is professor emeritus of psychology, and former associate dean of the School of Health and Life Sciences at Chapman University in Orange, CA. Eifert is an internationally recognized author, scientist, speaker, and trainer in the use of ACT. He is coauthor of *The Mindfulness and Acceptance Workbook for Anxiety*, *Anxiety Happens*, and *The Anorexia Workbook*.

Find your calm on the go—whenever anxiety happens

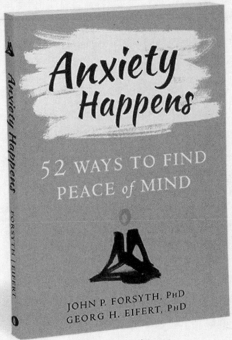

978-1684031108 / $14.95

This powerful, portable guide is packed with 52 in-the-moment mindfulness strategies you can use anytime, anywhere to soothe anxiety and find peace of mind.